The Merry Winter Time.

Words by Mrs. S. L. HOWELL.

Music by J. M. STILLMAN.

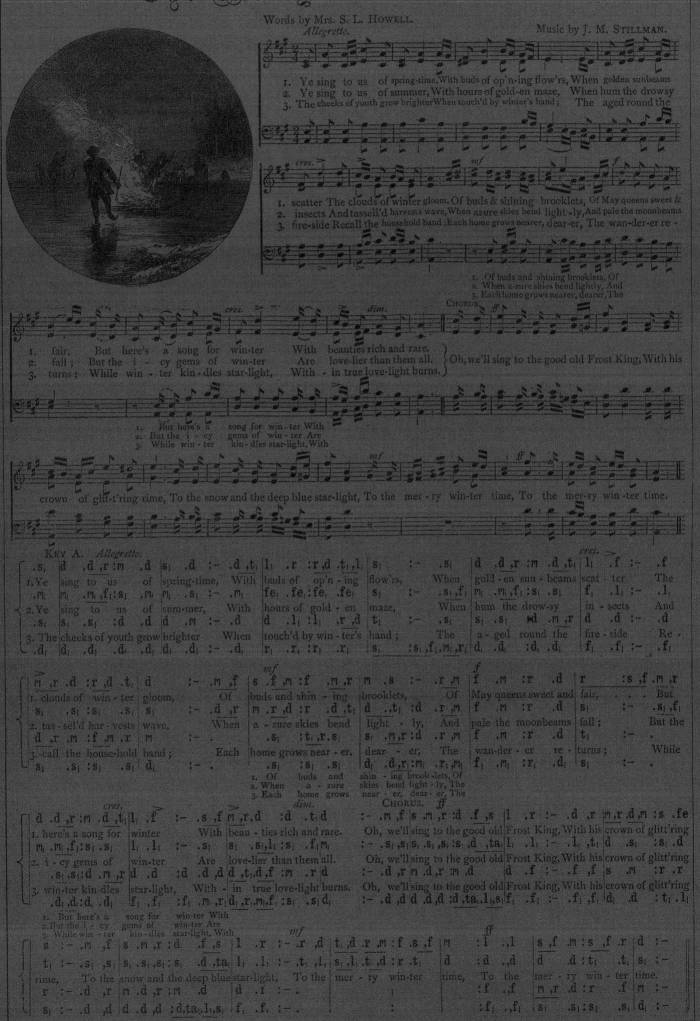

Allegretto.

1. Ye sing to us of spring-time, With buds of op'n-ing flow'rs, When golden sunbeams
2. Ye sing to us of summer, With hours of gold-en maze, When hum the drowsy
3. The cheeks of youth grow brighter When touch'd by winter's hand; The aged round the

1. scatter The clouds of winter gloom, Of buds & shining brooklets, Of May queens sweet &
2. insects And tassell'd harvests wave, When azure skies bend light-ly, And pale the moonbeams
3. fire-side Recall the household band; Each home grows nearer, dear-er, The wan-der-er re-

1. Of buds and shining brooklets, Of
2. When a-zure skies bend lightly, And
3. Each home grows nearer, dearer, The

1. fair, But here's a song for win-ter With beauties rich and rare.
2. fall; But the i-cy gems of win-ter Are love-lier than them all.
3. turns; While win-ter kin-dles star-light, With-in true love-light burns.

Oh, we'll sing to the good old Frost King, With his

1. But here's a song for win-ter With
2. But the i-cy gems of win-ter Are
3. While win-ter kin-dles star-light, With

crown of glitt'ring rime, To the snow and the deep blue star-light, To the mer-ry win-ter time, To the mer-ry win-ter time.

KEY A. *Allegretto.*

.s,	d .d,r:m .d	s, .d :- .d,t,	l, .r :r,d,t,l,	s, :- .s,	d .d,r:m .d,t,	l, .f :- .f
1.Ye	sing to us of	spring-time, With	buds of op'n-ing	flow'rs, When	gold-en sun-beams	scat-ter The
.m,	m, .m,f,:s, .m,	m, .m, .s, :- .m,	fe, .fe,:fe, .fe,	s, :- .s,,f,	m, .m,f,:s, .s,	f, .l, :- .l,
2.Ye	sing to us of sum-mer, With	hours of gold-en	maze, When	hum the drow-sy	in-sects And
.s,	s, .s, :d .d	d .m :- .d	d .l, :l, r,d	t, :- .s,	s, .s, :d .m,r	d .d :- .d
3. The checks of youth grow brighter When	touch'd by win-ter's	hand; The	a-ged round the	fire-side Re-
.d,	d, .d, :d, .d,	d, .d, :- .d,	r, .r :r, .r,	s, :s,,f,,m,r,	d, .d, :d .d,	f, .f, :- .f,

m ,r .d :r,d .t,	d :- .m ,f	s .f ,m:f .m,r	m .s :- .r,m	f .m :r .d	r :s ,f.m ,r
1. clouds of win-ter	gloom, Of	buds and shin-ing	brooklets, Of	May queens sweet and	fair, . . . But
s, .s, :s, .s,	s, :- .d,r	m .r,d:r .d,t,	d .,t, :d .r,m	f .m :r .d	s, :- .s,,f,
2. tas-sel'd har-vests	wave, When	a-zure skies bend	light-ly, And	pale the moonbeams	fall; . . . But the
d ,r .m :f,m,r	m :- .	.s, :t,,r.s,	s, .m,r:d .r,m	f .m :r .d	t, :- .
3.-call the house-hold	band; Each	home grows near-er,	dear-er, The	wan-der-er re-	turns; While
s, .s, :s, .s,	d, :- .	.s, :s, .s,	d, .d,r:m, .r,m,	f, .m, :r, .d,	s, :- .

1. Of buds and shin-ing brook-lets, Of
2. When a-zure skies bend light-ly, The
3. Each home grows near-er, dear-er, The

CHORUS. *ff*

d .d,r:m .d,t,	l, .f :- .s ,f.m,r.d :d .t,d	:- .m ,f	s .m,r:d .f,s	l .r :- .d,r	m,r.d,m :s .fe
1. here's a song for	winter With beau-ties rich and rare.	Oh, we'll sing to the good old	Frost King, With his	crown of glitt'ring
m, .m,f,:s, .s,	l, .l, :- .s,	s, .s,,l,:s, .f,m,	:- .s,,s,s, .s, ,s,:s .d ,ta,	l, .l, :- .l, ,t,	d .s, :s .d
2. i-cy gems of	win-ter Are love-lier than them all.	Oh, we'll sing to the good old	Frost King, With his	crown of glitt'ring
.s,,s,:d .m,r	d .d :d .d,d	d,.t,d,f:m .r,d	:- .d ,r m,d.r:m .d	d .f :- .f ,f	s .m :r .r
3. win-ter kin-dles	star-light, With-in true love-light burns.	Oh, we'll sing to the good old	Frost King, With his	crown of glitt'ring
.d,,d,:d, .d,	f, .f, :f,.m,r,d	r,.m,f:s, .s,d,	:- .d ,d d,.d,d, :d .ta,.l,,s,	f, .f, :- .f ,f,d	d .d :t, .l,

1. But here's a song for win-ter With
2. But the i-cy gems of win-ter Are
3. While win-ter kin-dles star-light, With

mf *ff*

s :- .m ,f	s .m,r:d .f,s	l .r :- .r ,d t,.d,r:m :f.s ,f.m	m :l .,l	s,f.m:s .f,r,d	d :-
t, :- .s, ,s,	s .s,s,:s .d,ta,	l, .l, :- .t, ,l, s,.l,t,d:r.t,	d :d .,d	d .d:t, .t, ,t,	s, :-
rime, To the	snow and the deep blue	star-light, To the	mer-ry win-ter	time, To the	mer-ry win-ter time.
r :- .d ,r	m .d,r:m .d	d .r:- .	:f.f	m,r.d:r .f :m	:-
s, :- .d ,d	d .d .d :d,ta,.l,,s,	f, .f, :- .	:f,.f,	s, .s,:s, .s,	d, :-

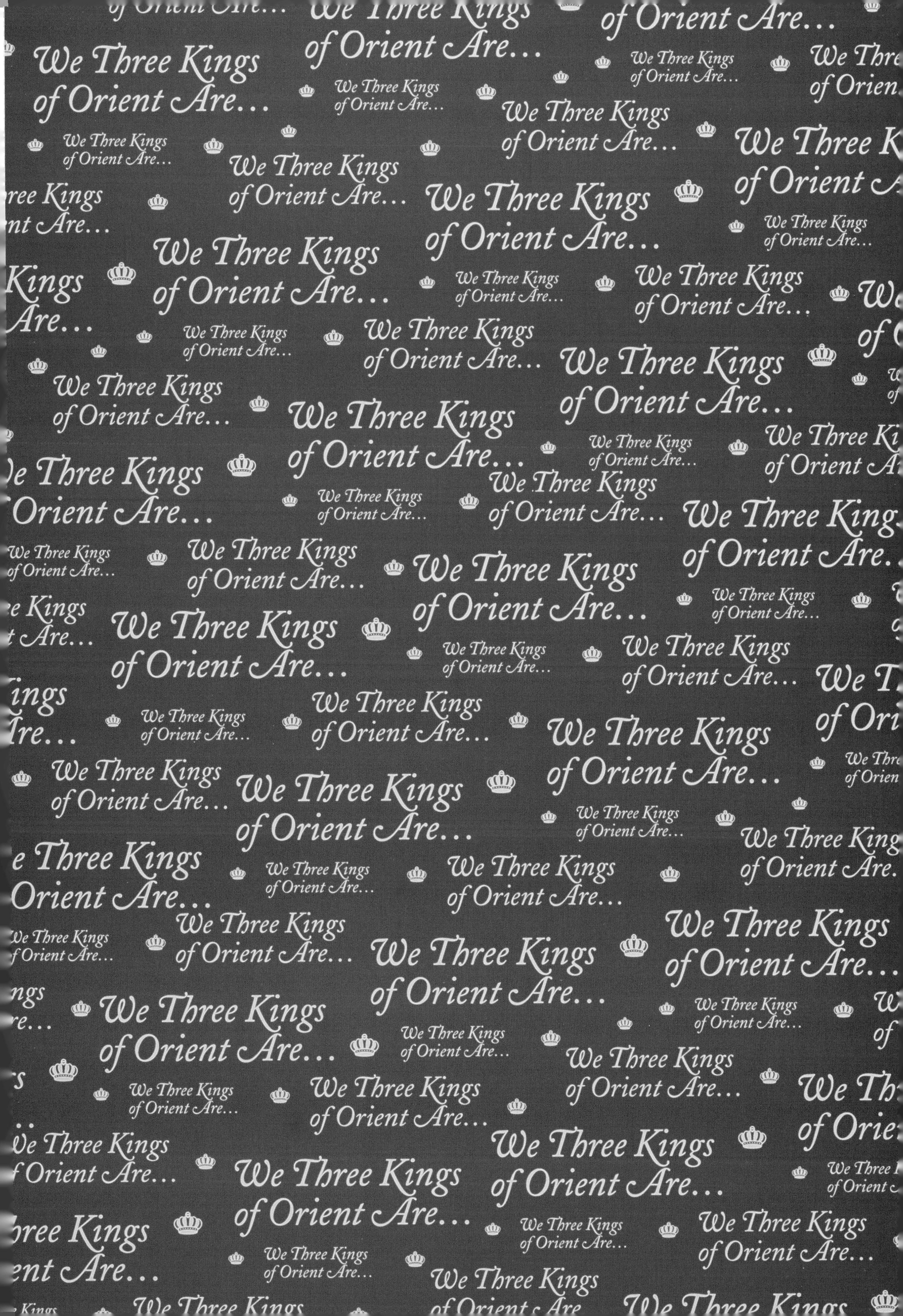
We Three Kings of Orient Are...

Merry Christmas…
& A Happy New Year

Merry Christmas…
& A Happy New Year

Merry Christmas…
& A Happy New Year

Merry Christmas…
& A Happy New Year

Merry Christmas…
& A Happy New Year

Merry Christmas…
& A Happy New Year

Merry Chr

& A Happ

Merry Christmas…
& A Happy New Year

Merry Christmas…
& A Happy New Year

Merry Christmas…
& A Happy New Year

Merry Christmas..
& A Happy New Y

…
New Year

Merry Christmas…
& A Happy New Year

Merry Christmas…
& A Happy New Year

Merry Christmas…
& A Happy New Year

Merry Chris
& A Happy

…
New Year

ry Christmas…
A Happy New Year

Merry Christmas…
& A Happy New Year

Merry Christmas…
& A Happy New Year

Merry Christmas…
& A Happy New Year

Merry Christmas…
& A Happy New Year

Merry Christmas..
& A Happy Ne

Merry Christmas…
& A Happy New Year

Merry Christmas…
& A Happy New Year

Merry Christmas…
& A Happy New Year

Merry Christmas…
& A Happy New Year

Merry Christmas…
& A Happy New Year

Merry Christmas.
& A Happy New

…
hristmas…
ppy New Year

Merry Christmas…
& A Happy New Year

Merry Christmas…
& A Happy New Year

Merry Christmas…
& A Happy New Year

Merry Christmas…
& A Happy New Year

Merry Christmas…
& A Happy New Year

Merry Christmas…
& A Happy New Year

Merry
& A Ha

…
Year

Merry Christmas…
& A Happy New Year

Merry Christmas…
& A Happy New Year

Merry Christmas…
& A Happy New Year

Merry Christmas.
& A Happy New Year

Merry Chr
& A Ha

Merry Christmas…
A Happy New Year

Merry Christmas…
& A Happy New Year

Merry Christmas…
& A Happy New Year

Merry Christmas…
& A Happy New Year

Merry Chri
& A

Merry Christmas…
& A Happy New Year

Merry Christmas…
& A Happy New Year

Merry Christmas…
& A Happy New Year

Merry Christmas.
& A Happy New Ye

s…
Merry Christmas…
& A Happy New Year

Merry Christmas…

Merry Christmas…
& A Happy New Year

Merry Christ

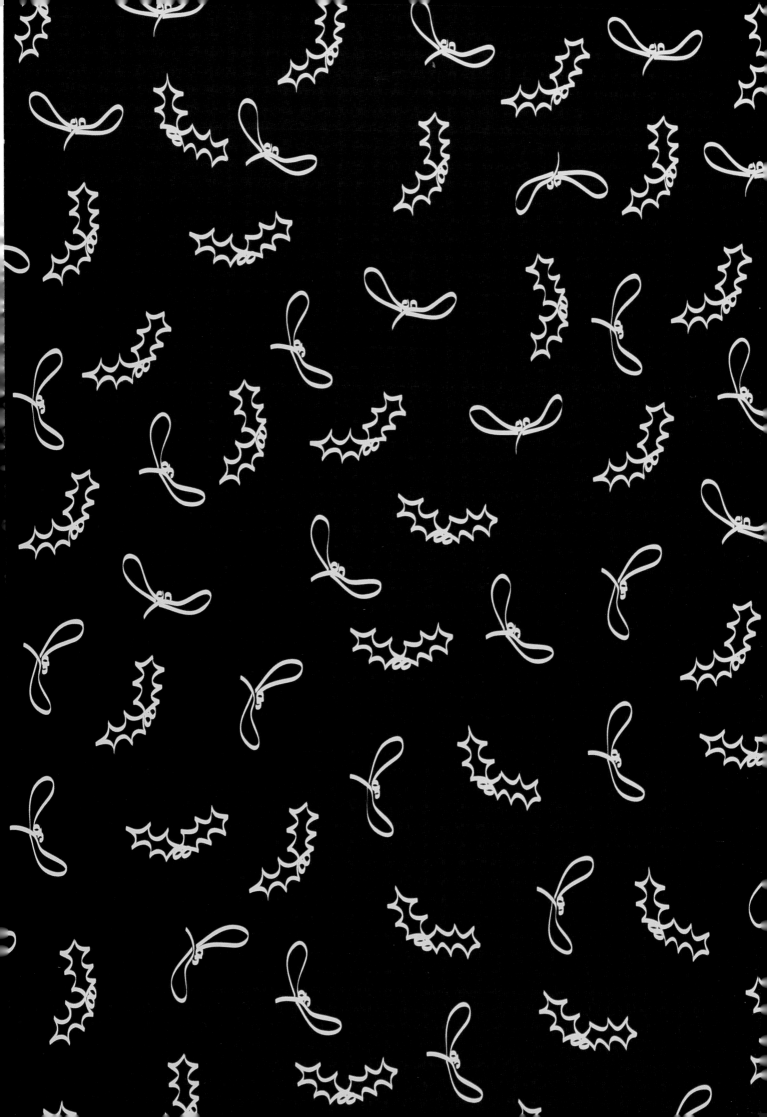

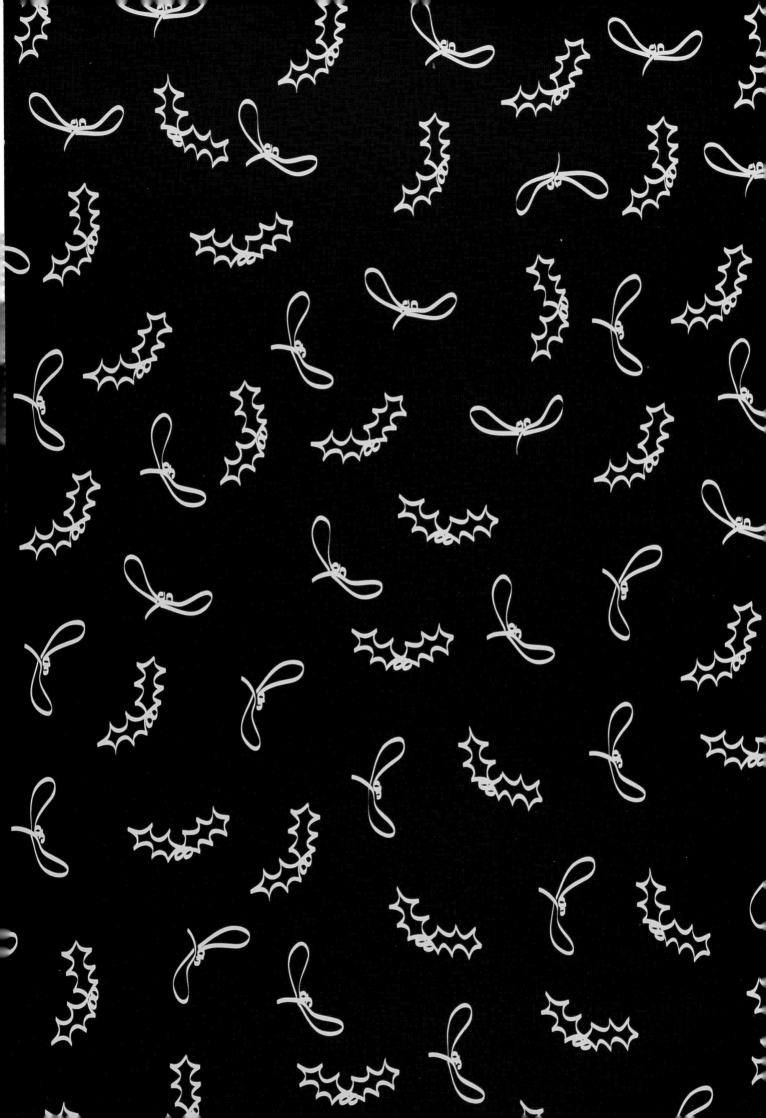

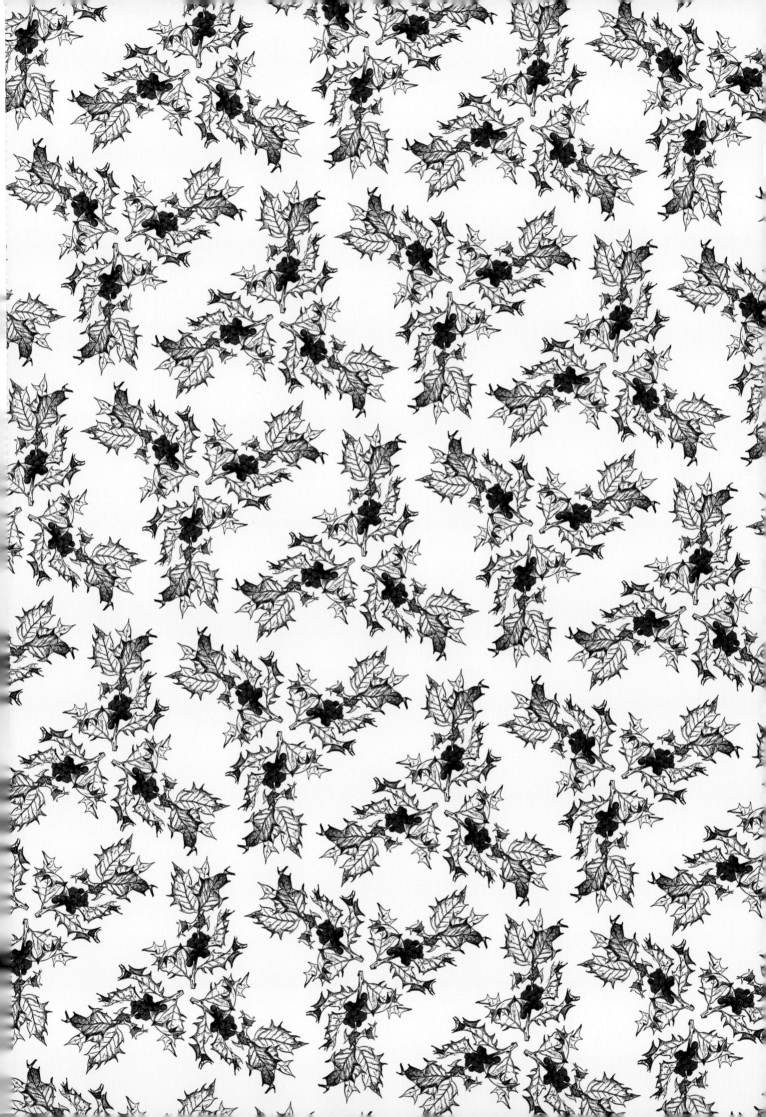

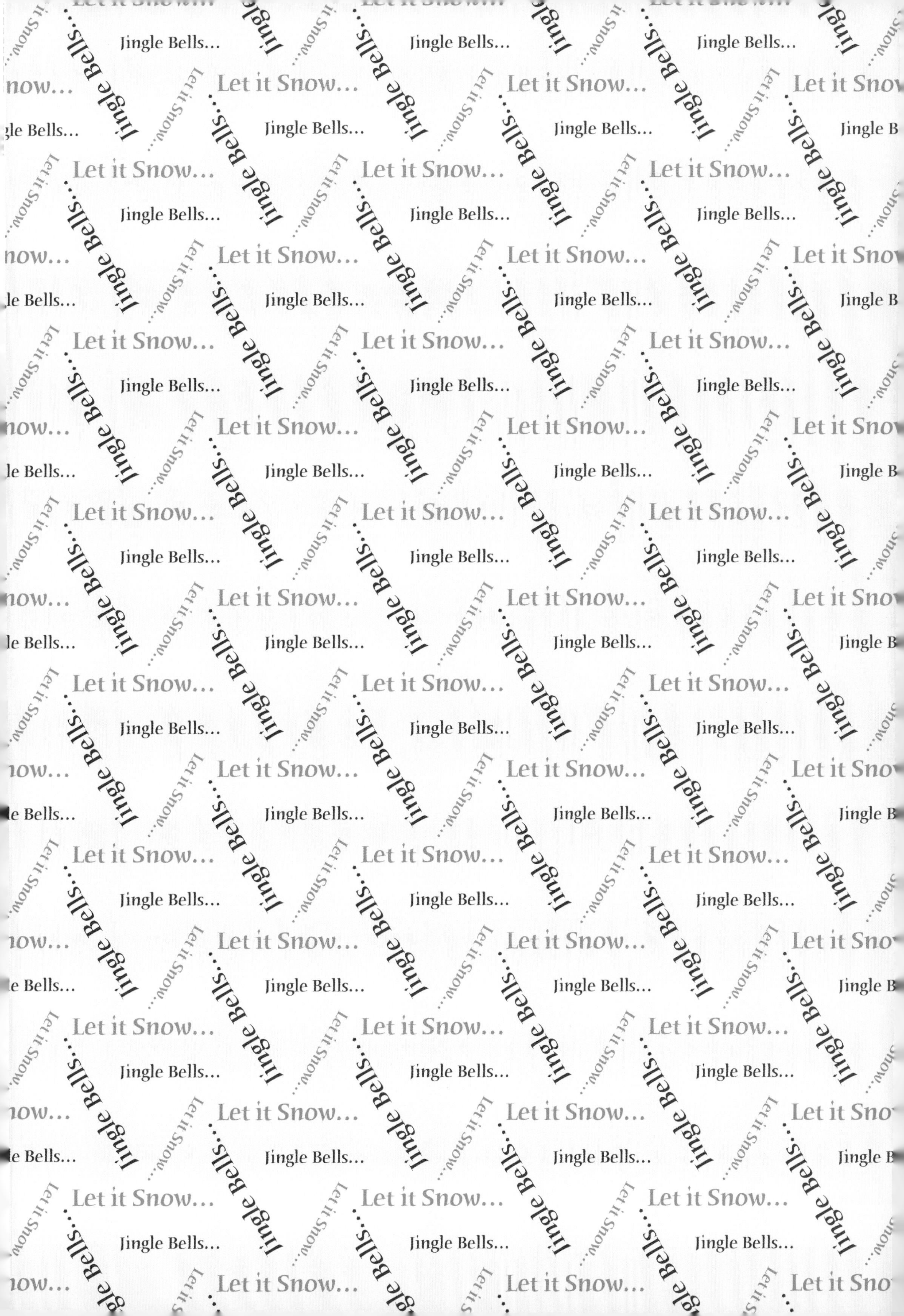
Jingle Bells…
Let it Snow…

And the angel said unto them, Fear not: for, behold, I bring you good tidings of great joy, which shall be to all people. For unto you is born this day in the city of David a Saviour, which is Christ the Lord.

And the angel said unto them, Fear not: for, behold, I bring you good tidings of great joy, which shall be to all people. For unto you is born this day in the city of David a Saviour, which is Christ the Lord.

And the angel said unto them, Fear not: for, behold, I bring you good tidings of great joy, which shall be to all people. For unto you is born this day in the city of David a Saviour, which is Christ the Lord.

And the angel said unto them, Fear not: for, behold, I bring you good tidings of great joy, which shall be to all people. For unto you is born this day in the city of David a Saviour, which is Christ the Lord.

And the angel said unto them, Fear not: for, behold, I bring you good tidings of great joy, which shall be to all people. For unto you is born this day in the city of David a Saviour, which is Christ the Lord.

And the angel said unto them, Fear not: for, behold, I bring you good tidings of great joy, which shall be to all people. For unto you is born this day in the city of David a Saviour, which is Christ the Lord.

And the angel said unto them, Fear not: for, behold, I bring you good tidings of great joy, which shall be to all people. For unto you is born this day in the city of David a Saviour, which is Christ the Lord.

And the angel said unto them, Fear not: for, behold, I bring you good tidings of great joy, which shall be to all people. For unto you is born this day in the city of David a Saviour, which is Christ the Lord.

And the angel said unto them, Fear not: for, behold, I bring you good tidings of great joy, which shall be to all people. For unto you is born this day in the city of David a Saviour, which is Christ the Lord.

And the angel said unto them, Fear not: for, behold, I bring you good tidings of great joy, which shall be to all people. For unto you is born this day in the city of David a Saviour, which is Christ the Lord.

And the angel said unto them, Fear not: for, behold, I bring you good tidings of great joy, which shall be to all people. For unto you is born this day in the city of David a Saviour, which is Christ the Lord.

I Saw Three Ships come Sailing by on Christmas Day, on Christmas Day, I Saw Three Ships come Sailing by on Christmas Day, in the Morning ❧ I Saw Three Ships come Sailing by on Christmas Day, on Christmas Day, I Saw Three Ships come Sailing by on Christmas Day, in the Morning ❧ I Saw Three Ships come Sailing by on Christmas Day, on Christmas Day, I Saw Three Ships come Sailing by on Christmas Day, in the Morning ❧ I Saw Three Ships come Sailing by on Christmas Day, on Christmas Day, I Saw Three Ships come Sailing by on Christmas Day, in the Morning ❧ I Saw Three Ships come Sailing by on Christmas Day, on Christmas Day, I Saw Three Ships come Sailing by on Christmas Day, in the Morning ❧ I Saw Three Ships come Sailing by on Christmas Day, on Christmas Day, I Saw Three Ships come Sailing by on Christmas Day, in the Morning ❧ I Saw Three Ships come Sailing by on Christmas Day, on Christmas Day, I Saw Three Ships come Sailing by on Christmas Day, in the Morning ❧ I Saw Three Ships come Sailing by on Christmas Day, on Christmas Day, I Saw Three Ships come Sailing by on Christmas Day, in the Morning ❧ I Saw Three Ships come Sailing by on Christmas Day, on Christmas Day, I Saw Three Ships come Sailing by on Christmas Day, in the Morning ❧ I Saw Three Ships come Sailing by on Christmas Day, on Christmas Day, I Saw Three Ships come Sailing by on Christmas Day, in the Morning ❧ I Saw Three Ships come Sailing by on Christmas Day, on Christmas Day, I Saw Three Ships come Sailing by on Christmas Day, in the Morning ❧ I Saw Three Ships come Sailing by on Christmas Day, on Christmas Day, I Saw Three Ships come Sailing by on Christmas Day, in the Morning ❧ I Saw Three Ships come Sailing by on Christmas Day, on Christmas Day, I Saw Three Ships come Sailing by on Christmas Day, in the Morning ❧ I Saw Three Ships come Sailing by on Christmas Day, on Christmas Day, I Saw Three Ships come Sailing by on Christmas Day, in the Morning ❧ I Saw Three Ships come Sailing by on Christmas Day, on Christmas Day, I Saw Three Ships come Sailing by on Christmas Day, in the Morning ❧ I Saw Three Ships come Sailing by on Christmas Day, on Christmas Day, I Saw Three Ships come Sailing by on Christmas Day, in the Morning ❧ I Saw Three Ships come Sailing by on Christmas Day, on Christmas Day, I Saw Three Ships come Sailing by on Christmas Day, in the Morning ❧ I Saw Three Ships come Sailing by on Christmas Day, on Christmas Day, I Saw Three Ships come Sailing by on Christmas Day, in the Morning ❧ I Saw Three Ships come Sailing by on Christmas Day, on Christmas Day, I Saw Three Ships come Sailing by on Christmas Day, in the Morning ❧ I Saw Three Ships come Sailing by on Christmas Day, on Christmas Day, I Saw Three Ships come Sailing by on Christmas Day, in the Morning ❧ I Saw Three Ships come Sailing by on Christmas Day, on Christmas Day, I Saw Three Ships come Sailing by on Christmas Day, in the Morning ❧ I Saw Three Ships come Sailing by on Christmas Day, on Christmas Day, I Saw Three Ships come Sailing by on Christmas Day, in the Morning ❧ I Saw Three Ships come Sailing by on Christmas Day, on Christmas Day, I Saw Three Ships come Sailing by on Christmas Day, in the Morning ❧ I Saw Three